www.finishinglinepress.com

IN HARMONY
WITH HOMOPHONES

a collection of poems written by

Mike Wahl

Finishing Line Press
Georgetown, Kentucky

IN HARMONY
WITH HOMOPHONES

ACKNOWLEDGMENTS

None of the poems in this collection have been previously published.
They are a result of words and phrases that God used to get and keep my
attention. I am deeply grateful for these and all other blessings that He has
bestowed on me.

Publisher: Leah Huete de Maines
Editor: Christen Kincaid
Cover Art: Mike Wahl—Christmas Eve 2019, at my farm
Author Photo: Xerxes Wahl
Cover Design: Elizabeth Maines McCleavy

Order online: www.finishinglinepress.com
            also available on amazon.com

Author inquiries and mail orders:
Finishing Line Press
P. O. Box 1626
Georgetown, Kentucky 40324
U. S. A.

Table of Contents

Introduction

This effort is titled *In Harmony With Homophones* because each poem meets specific guidelines of construction, using homophones as focal points. By definition, the term "homophone" is used to describe a word that sounds the same as another word but has a different meaning and spelling. For each of these poems, homophone-paired words appear as the first and last words, and where three different words have the same sound, the third spelling appears somewhere in the middle of that poem. Very simple examples might be the poems: "See the sea" and "Si, I see the sea". When speaking of harmony in other than musical terms, it refers to peaceful coexistence and compatibility of thoughts. Homophones aren't normally pegged into this kind of association, since most paired words that sound the same have entirely different meanings that can be disharmonious. A particularly extreme example is the pair: raise & raze, which in terms of infrastructure, have exactly opposite meanings.

Because the poem titles are the homophones themselves, they provide clues as to possible poem contents and contexts. However, just because the reader knows the first and last words, before the actual reading occurs, it doesn't mean the poem's essence will be anything like what might be expected. Some poems in the collection are sequential in subject, though not physically adjacent, so have fun tying them together in your own mind. Some poems that are physically sequential are related to previous poems because of the use of the same word in a poem being used as a homophone title in the next entry. I am hopeful that this will provide poetic harmony throughout the book.

Writing poems may seem to be a strange side-line for someone like me, a farmer. However, if you consider poems to be like weeds, in that they can grow anywhere, and may acquire any manner of prickliness or beauty, as is their nature, then I self-qualify to write them. For me, poems seem to flourish more succulently in a rural setting, as they have more opportunities to savor such a wide and unconstrained environment on their way to maturity. The poems in this collection explore subtleties of various aspects of rural living, religion, politics, and relationships. Often ideas for poems occur as I go about my daily tasks in the garden or around the farm, demanding to be written down. For those instances, I carry a pen and paper in my pocket for scribbling down those lines, before I forget.

These poems tend to be short, and contained within a single page, so that the reader's attention can stay focused. They were made in America for your convenience and reading pleasure. In a way, we're all farmers, harvesting what we can from where life reigns. May all your homophones live in harmony, forever after.

I'll—Aisle—Isle

I'll have to admit
there are detours I should have taken,
when instead,
I plowed through barricades
and investigated obstacles unworthy
of my attention;

I would like to think I could improve my reputation,
if I could only find a suitable solution,
and certainly,
with all the shelves so sumptuously stocked,
the mega-store of life's solutions
could help fulfill my quest,
but I'm agonizing over which aisle
to instigate a search,
unsure if I've correctly diagnosed
my image as two-faced,
or if the photograph is merely blurred.

Ideally, I would like to send condolences to anyone
who has been a victim of my recklessness,
and I would write with contrition in someone else's
suggested words, one thousand times,
on a chalkboard during recess;

but perhaps there is no room available
for an avalanche of full regret,
with my reach too short for that tall shelf,
and my best approach might be to seek seclusion
on some deserted and forgotten isle.

Bolder—Boulder

Bolder than he had ever been before,
having been hardened by improper accusations
that threatened his utmost veracity,
he spoke loudly against the usurpation
of privacy and individual rights;
the Constitution had been bypassed
until there was barely any freedom left,
so his silencers locked his protests
behind the thick walls of the jailhouse.

They said he had a soapbox,
but it was too tall for one man to climb;
still, no one brought a ladder
or offered to help him with the words,
spoken
(with careful and righteous thought)
against the usurpers who were bigger than he;
so they squelched his revolution
before it could gain ground,
and buried the whole affair deep beneath
the bureaucracy that was like
an immovable massive boulder.

Passed—Past

Passed-over concepts compete
with our real failures to see
which has the lowest level of remorse;
somehow, neither wins, but both get a prize;
other times, our failed agendas
fulfill themselves as someone else's dreams,
without us ever knowing,
and leaving us missing out on success,
or adulation;
it is an answer with too few knowns
to be adequately addressed.

Who knows then if we can conveniently
locate an acceptance of a previously
disputed artifact that never
found favor until it linked
a misunderstood today
with a completely clear yesterday?
We might as well be content to say
it is a muddling of uncertainties
that confuses everything with postulates
that can't even begin
to define an unknown past.

We've—Weave

We've secluded ourselves
against the wind as best we could,
in the developing darkness,
piling rocks around the edges
of the narrow depression that once held roots,
now tilted and still enclosed by earth,
but on the wrong side of the wind.

It howls furiously, as if searching for death—
it had come, Chinook-like,
before exposing its full fury,
suddenly announcing itself only briefly
with a harsh cold gust that tumbled me
backwards down onto the rocks.

It's just the dog, Shep, and I,
seeking the stray cattle that must have
somehow known to seek their own shelter
against the coming storm.
Shep and I will share each other's heat
during the night as the wind
tries to grab it for its own.

They will be worried back at the ranch-house,
but there is no way for them to know
my horse has fled and I am in the wrong part
of the world than I intended,
stranded with this mangled leg and useless hand.
She will sit at her loom,
it is her solace at times of distress,
shuttling thoughts that she can't weave.

Hear—Here

Hear well, you children of difficult times,
there is misery in the company you keep,
and the scales are unbalanced against you;
ferret out the secrets that
are the blocks building walls
between the withering of wisdom
and the golden rules of hearts
that keep you safely here.

Allowed—Aloud

Allowed certain privileges
as a result of her connections,
abuse soon became an obvious consequence,
where she considered herself beyond punishment.
She would henceforth be a Someone,
immune to ordinary influences;
Someone turned my angst into an agony,
far past the trepidations
of an unwelcoming doormat,
stepping past old thresholds only
as far as the familiar room,
but no farther because there now
was no curiosity if other rooms existed.
Someone behaved illogically,
as if nothing else belonged in the space,
narrowing the options to include only
the way it's always been done,
because the box has never been opened,
much less used to invoke any
extracurricular intellectual activity.
Someone flipped ideologies
like there was a need to escape a hot griddle,
closing inclinations to amend a past repertoire,
and encapsulating future advances
into words that would most likely
be a conversation never spoken aloud.

Rapt—Wrapped

Rapt attentions sometimes get spanned
across an abyss that exceeds normal expectations,
where one tends to take for granted
that idiosyncrasies won't turn into pet peeves.
Pardon me, your slip is showing.

Things that aren't resolved by sundown
sometimes have to wait until 2:00 AM,
ticking away minutes of misunderstandings
that thought they'd withstood the test of time,
when it was merely clock hands that didn't move.

Offering apologies is a grueling undertaking,
not like death, but sometimes just as hard
as digging your own grave,
knowing you've run out of all the spices
intended to keep your eternity well wrapped.

Bad—Bade

"bad" fits well between "good" and "ugly",
but it stays unaffected by the slot,
as long as it involves maneuvers
intent on exploiting human weaknesses.

I am enthralled by your willingness
to involve your true intentions,
complete with inherent frailties,
boding well for our mutual existence,
where honesty plays the trump card
that keeps the game
suspended until all
the havoc has been wreaked,
and before the deadline
advances into a forfeit.

I favor your refusal to be beckoned
into a useless silence
that is the only bridge
readily reaching the other side,
where waits a noxious disposition to demonstrate
the meaning of an unwelcome tomorrow,
as desolation dwells in isolation
captured by a despair where
each farewell has already been bade.

Dammed-Damned

Dammed up from the flow of progress
because of hypocrisies of bureaucrats
who delve into delays like they
must take their lunch break right now,
are the waters of inequality that trickle
slowly into the pond that grows ever larger,
where regulations serve as refuse
to reinforce the dam that inhibits
the flow of social justice,
and as a consequence,
also holding back the gathering agitations
stirred into those impeded waters
that should have been left to their
slow trickles of release, gently,
unrelated to the resolution
that those inciting all the turmoil
will one day be the damned.

Disgust—Discussed

Disgust finally won the conclusion,
a victory over *hope springs eternal.*
There were the battles that prolonged
the conflict over many decades:
off and on; in and out; up and down;
with no real way to resolve
the boundaries that veered both ways,
just useless tugging,
like trying to find anti-gravity.
Hope goes haphazardly
    down a wrong-way road;
Hope goes hog-wild
    over a worthless trinket;
Hope goes hay-wire
    across borders of intended neglect;
Hope gains employment
    where there never is a salary;
Hope hints at instances
    that dissolve into nebulosity;
Hope goes into hiding
    fearing the fate of imprisonment;
Hope gathers into crevasses
    like dust and lint of distrust;
When all of the figures tally into a bottom line,
it all adds into zero,
where nothing is the only thing
still being discussed.

Fair—Fare

Fair weather sometimes finds solace
with a red sunset,
portended without any real reason,
except solitude easily accepts rainbows
as substitutes for storm clouds;

if you find yourself sharing the wrong story
that crops itself at the edges
before it needs to bleed
onto another page,
it is apt to coalesce its version of red
into a private sunset,
as quick anger displaces more
than a slower trust.

You hear about win/win situations,
but they don't come along that often,
especially if you don't go searching—
then, too, there's always some sort of price,
and the best thing to do is negotiate;

if your suns go down too many times
into cloud-banks of colorless uncaring,
it may be time to buy up whatever
left-over bedraggled rainbow you can retrieve.
Go ahead and turn back the page you once saved,
and go begging for a return trip ticket
no matter what the fare.

Some—Sum

Some of the things we take for granted
as unchangeable boundaries
may be only assumptions;
here I consider proof of my existence,
coming as hard-fought, hard-won,
not because I can't pinch myself,
or get someone else to administer pain,
but philosophical truth demands more;

my existence can't be real until my
surroundings have been verified by an
external definition that provides
reimbursement for the debts that I accumulate;
it cannot be one that stays nebulous,
refusing all interviews and public comments
by a pretext of ignorance;
I would simply never know, nor care,
if parameters shifted inside my influence
unless there was an outside observer
retaining a permanent point of reference.

Chronology too easily convolutes itself
into yesterdays of twenty years ago or then
into tomorrows that only happen if no other
existence preempts the given structure,
better known as dreams;
true existence finds itself defined
when its conversion into another potential option
has no merit unless it's been predetermined
that it won't accumulate any false advocate,
and thus no matter how many
different ways you add columns,
His totality always arrives at the same Sum.

One—Won

One minute is as good as any other,
none being able to advance the clock
differently than what parameters provide.
Love changes directions indiscriminately,
scooting along the bench until
I get forced off the edge,
received by gravity,
but deceived by air that is
pretending to be substance.
Until something shifts outside the park,
all the benches stay occupied
by derelicts that pre-existed as roses.
Outside the park is a halo of innocence
that pretends it has no interest in benches,
or even cares if gravity has won.

Tiers—Tears

Tiers that once segregated
loneliness from patience
retreat into a hodgepodge of residues,
bringing forward new-found prospects
that I could fit comfortably
within the angle of your zone:

variable, like mine,
that mixes into moods
of distracted anarchy;

intense as the purposes
that underline what I have
already high-lighted;

invigorating adventures
as inspiring as any realm
of Greek mythology;

rushing to undo infractions,
so to meet the criticality
of silence with its gold;

leaving perplexity
to find its own way home
in a darkness slick with tears.

Patience—Patients

Patience places itself at our disposal
in ways we may not recognize,
being too busy with all the other things;
until situations progress to a realization
that there is absolutely nothing more
that can be done,
and we must conform to uselessness;

we are anxiously fermenting plans
that have no chance of being implemented.
When there is nothing else left,
resignation invades comprehension:
there the path splits,
one way with proper discernment
leads to an introspection of acceptance;
the other direction defiles itself
with despondency and depression,
assigning despair into institutions
where residues reside as patients.

Mail—Male

Mail boxes sitting on posts
are positioning themselves towards obsolescence.
Deliver us from evil.
Incoming. Ring tone or vibration?
Text or message, words or voice?
Wherever your computer fits best,
in hand, spanning knees, or desk-bound,
mailboxes are full of themselves, over-flowed,
stuffed like a turkey full of goodies,
but also burdened
with bones to pick around.

Deleting bills doesn't diminish debt—
(yes, less licking envelopes and sticking stamps)
just pay on-line and go green
without ever dispensing green from your wallet.

Of course, there's left-over SPAM,
enough to fill its own folder,
by following forwards and ignoring
no-phishing allowed signs.

Finding surprise replies
helps detour around excuses that demand no mandates
(like neither rain, nor sleet, nor snow)
to enhance our electronic mailboxes.

Time to minimize any perceived discrepancies
of referring to the carrier as a MAILMAN,
where the bringer of our written correspondence
is most likely not even male.

Fowl—Foul

Fowl of all sorts reach a debilitating
level of activity as darkness descends,
unable to function even
with threats of eminent death—
they become easy prey
when the chickens come home to roost;
although the first hint of daylight
restarts stalled metabolisms,
nothing dawns inside their feeble heads
at the far end of a day.

The ducks apparently believe the middle
of the driveway should be a safe zone,
as that's where the normally protective mama
clusters her ducklings,
yet she readily abandons them
to approaching vehicles,
having learned by experience
that size really does matter,
and tires are better fled than fought—
it seems a lesson worth propagating,
but perhaps not for mama ducks.

The duck crossing sign carries no guarantees
that everything will pause for small objects
that are the same color as the gravel,
yet the mail carrier,
on her way to deliver a package,
does dutifully stop;
still, the ducklings are rambling
instead of scrambling to cross,
breaking the rule of the sign
originally made in their favor,
a deserving fit for a foul.

Blue—Blew

Blue flames signaled that the heat
was at an elevation that had escalated
before we'd had a chance to cool—
we burned the categories
we had thought were safe,
flinging oxygen and fuel
at the spark that had been connived
from some trivial diversion,
thinking even all the embers had
long ago been extinguished
on a telltale moonless night;

as the flames fanned higher,
our self-deceptions were reversing
previous perceptions and expectations
that there could be a reduction
back to a level assigned to a candle wick,
a more deserving status
of this destructive flame,
where once,
differences could easily have been resolved,
depending simply on which way we blew.

Pain—Pane

Pain drains the color from his face.
He fights for consciousness
at the urging of some inner command,
demanding that he stop the flow of blood
that tries to squeeze beneath his belt,
now newly reborn as a tourniquet,
beyond which that leg measures loss,
and too, the mangled hand finds no solace
in their sheaths of congealing blood.

Somehow, he is an outside observer,
as if there is a window
of a different perspective,
blurring details and tinting perceptions
of opportunity, as only a vision can do.
To everything there is a season,
a time to die,
and a time to be born.
It is a straining to see
through the glass darkly,
to gain a further comprehension
of what lies beyond that darkened pane.

Seams—Seems

Seams of daylight formed between
the un-stitched but tightly packed
eastern stratus clouds,
but made no further headway;
I was equally incapacitated,
as every slight movement sent a
severe reminder of my broken leg
and mutilated hand;
my faithful Shep had
whimpered and cried,
but I finally convinced him
he must go home alone.

Hunger and thirst had plagued us both
since yesterday,
when my spooked horse abandoned us;
I didn't know if he could find his way home,
but I knew Shep could,
and would return with help,
even if it might be too late.

He could cover the miles fast,
an urgency he sensed,
as my strength faltered;
in semi-delirium I pondered
how easily our comfort zones could leave us,
especially when least expected,
and through the fuzziness I thought
I heard the barking of Shep,
mingled with her calling out my name,
but things aren't always so predictable,
and rescue not as simple as it seems.

Rights—Rites—Writes

Rights and wrongs
differentiate how our paths
lead us into temptations
that we may refuse, if they are unfamiliar,
but more likely we will accept them,
if it's what everyone else is doing.

Standards seem too willing to dissolve
themselves into shallow shadows
that can no longer be pinned
to proper origins.

When decisions demand that we define
the rites that point us either
towards straight and narrow,
or deflect us into random chaos
that we mistake for civilization,
we drag feet to prolong our demise,
but slowly fade into acceptance of evil.
We can choose to use words to boost
our image, or define the truth,
but ultimately, our actions tend to further
retract our testimonies;
then, like it or not,
it defaults to an admission
that we have no commitment to any of the words
that have been written with wisdom,
and thus we'll live where the recourse
is only what the demon writes.

It's—Its

It's going to take a long time,
but we can annihilate the northern wilderness;
we can warm the tundra
into soybean fields, with no trees or deer
to interfere with production.
Antarctica can keep the ice-locked land
under miles of snow that we'll ship
from the north pole,
as we re-balance temperature equations,
making room in the northern hemisphere
for all the immigrants that need a new ideology;
transcontinental superhighways
across northern Canada and Russia
will invigorate the sprouting of municipalities
that will soon need even bigger by-passes
to circumvent rush-hours;

It won't be easy,
but we can give up winter sports
and moose hunting.

It will be a massive undertaking,
but we need to find a more attractive substitute
for replacing subzero Centigrades
with something even more astounding
than the brutal frigid reputation
that is so uniquely its.

Plain—Plane

Plain unveilings inadequately explain
the depths of depressions
where edges wedge themselves
into the last remaining crevasses of hope,
as if the final chance to achieve restitution
could fracture at any instant,
claiming the remainder of vitality;

To reassemble some semblance of satisfaction,
we must overcome the vulnerabilities
of alternate exploratory excursions
along the ledges,
slick with spilled failures,
and never assume there will be enough energy
left inside to automatically lift
ourselves from the depths
back onto a higher plane.

Chaste—Chased

Chaste and virtuous symmetries
attach themselves to her by mere
customary habits of their existence,
refusing to yield to a tenacious scattering
of abundant deceptions,
falsely describing themselves
as nothing better ever being available;

thus, with everything configured
towards a refined environment,
confined, but without a cage,
she waits by her unlit lamp,
confident that when the time is right
there will be abundant oil
to burn away the darkness of depravity.

He too knows the pitfalls of the darkness,
but never stumbles against the boulders
shoved by crude ignorance into the path—
there is a consuming intention to persevere,
being totally unconflicted towards
a resolution of ultimate discretion;

he has never circulated himself
amongst the wanton disasters of entanglements,
rather shredding evidence that
came from dark corners,
thus seeking his own narrow confinement,
until welcomed into a circle of her sudden lamplight,
secure in this new circumstance,
without a threat of ever being chased.

Piece—Peace

Piece-by-piece the tractor gets dismantled,
first shedding sheet metal
to expose entanglements of wires,
hoses, and hydraulic lines;
somewhere in that messy mass
is the cracked housing of the steering valve
that has unduly spewed forth
hydraulic fluid so effectively
that everything I touch now slickly
ignores my grasp as I am trying to decipher
what can be pushed aside
and what has to be disconnected or removed.

The tractor is age-crusted, well-worn,
and way past prime,
but heretofore faithful,
so this effort is to save it from the scrapyard.
If the pump is the heart of the hydraulic system,
this valve would be the lungs,
with multiple lines going both into and out
of its massiveness meant to contain 3000 psi.
Connections are around corners and ornery with age,
but I am equally obstinate,
as days turn into weeks.

My tools are coarse and hefty,
but like a surgeon's scalpel and scissors,
must be used to dissect intricacies
that were not designed for easy removal.
Being a part-time tractor doctor
means I can breathe without a mask,
start a new approach without washing my hands,
and not worry if I disconnect parts out of order.
Working on tractor ailments is tough,
but at least mistakes won't cause death,
which is what most brings me peace.

Might—Mite

Might not each enormous elephant
benefit by the adjacent association
of all the others close at hand,
(safety in numbers sort of thing?),
unless, of course, they don't
recognize each other as equals,
or concur that size doesn't really matter;
a mouse, they say, can frighten an elephant
because their warped point of reference
doesn't define a difference
between small and large,
(unlike humans who SHOULD distinguish?),
so everything strange becomes a threat,

so there is no solution to be found,
even if one could start over,
and work upward,
starting in the proximity of the smallest mite.

Hi—High

Hi or *hello* greetings come from everyone
we meet along the trails to the waterfalls.
October in Michigan's Upper Peninsula
means driving through miles
of forests where branches form
brilliantly leaved arches and tunnels;
those roads intersperse with multiplicities
of tumultuous rivers that are spilling
their tannin-tinted contents
over massive ledges and down steep cascades,
to tumble even more liquid abundance
into the volume of Lake Superior.
Some people willingly relinquish driving
through the splendiferous expanses
long enough to walk the kaleidoscopic paths,
to see and hear how the riotous rivers
obstinately obey gravity with their stunning displays
and ambiances of ubiquitous mists;
Those people are friendly folks,
happy participants of life,
who smile and speak when passing.
They may go back home to be grumpy,
without saying a word to their
urban neighboring counterparts,
but on the trail,
they are transiently human again.
It's not that there are rules
or special guidelines on how we
should behave in the out-lands,
versus for our metropolitan lives,
but rather, that the sharing of a thin secret
establishes a temporary camaraderie of exuberance,
knowing each is invigorated by nature's majesty;
there is an expectation and exultation
that all who walk those trails
will recognize themselves as more human,
and for now, along with you,
will hold their heads up high.

Roe—Row

Roe doesn't always dress-up
as fancy as caviar;
it tends to stay plain and smelly
when not covered up by smoke;
and champagne;

at the thought of fish eggs
mixed into his scrambled eggs,
my uncle never turns up his nose,
but he sure does
when his neighbor never says hello;

their property line
stays like a demilitarized zone,
where no one treads,
tending to stay plain and smelly,
as the hedging grows thick,
almost like sentries
stationed in a row.

In—Inn

In a less humble setting,
she said she was the best thing that
ever happened to me—
I tended to agree,
but felt reluctant to feed that ego;

accounting for the narrow misses,
and understating phases in the porosity of life,
love had leaked through;

engaging my attentions had required
a dedication less desirable than
a pet rock or a spider collection,
but tenacity was her strong suit,
and perseverance kept her
organized against defeat;

in the end,
determining how best to measure
the definition of a treasure
falls into the crevice of realization
that the only thing keeping
two frayed edges tied together
is the One who was born
on the night there was no room at the inn.

Based—Baste

Based on the ways we live our lives,
there seems little room to expand our agendas
into anything other than frustration.
When you're treading against the currents
of a vast ocean of despair,
if you reach for the false buoyancies
of catastrophes and atrocities,
you will surely drown.

Smelling roses is someone's solution.
It is what it is, she said, but no one smiled.
There are no easy solutions
tendered to teach swimming through mud—
you have to learn the breathing pattern
on your own.
Breathing is most successful
when you make it your first priority.

After that lesson has been mastered,
make my next objective an island,
beached far beyond the breakers
where time only matters
to the sun-soaked sand,
as a reminder to turn occasionally,
and slather lotion,
just to baste.

Ways—Weighs

Ways intended for me
are apparently chosen differently
than how they are for others,
with commonality a rare occurrence;
trudge with me just one day
through the random pitfalls
that somehow always get rescheduled
to fit my sad disclosures
of black and white monologues,
sandwiched between
haphazard and catastrophe;
it is my lot in life
to strive against the ice-jams
that keep pushing more and more
with the spring-time thaw,
like rushing new releases into box-offices
still closed due to held-over winter block-busters;
just as huge ice chunks pile themselves
into narrow constraints,
there is a stacking of obstacles,
against me, always higher,
merely because they are slightly lighter
than what life weighs.

Reining—Reigning—Raining

Reining in of deplorable memories
sometimes requires merely waiting
on the advancement of age,
where the eroding of sharp edges
waylays new jagged cuts and bruising battles;

still, how can memories of those things
we wish now had never happened,
keep reigning as perturbations
on an otherwise smooth curve
of impeccable existence?

indeed, why do pleasant epochs
fade so quickly from their significance,
only to be readily replaced by tempests
of past disappointing indiscretions,
down-poured into persistent raining?

By—Buy—Bye

By 6:30 AM she is ready
for the adventures of a new day.
Patiently she waits for me
at my side of the bed,
waiting for my time to rise.
Already, with her nose,
she has pushed her bed
under the edge of this larger one,
for daytime storage.
When again approaches her bedtime,
she will pull it back out
and carefully smooth away the wrinkles.

This morning,
I know she has already actuated
the foot switch for opening the doggy door,
allowing her access to the outside
for her morning duties;
similarly, she has made her return, quietly,
so she won't disturb me.
Hers is a loyalty I could never buy.

The years she has been such a great
part of my life are too many
to accurately account,
since she just appeared one day,
bedraggled and mal-nourished.
I am reluctant to discuss
her age with anyone,
lest it refresh the threat
that the time will be forthcoming
for that disastrous day
when my remaining recourse
will be to say my last good bye.

Rome—Roam

Rome built itself to one day
rule the known world,
without thinking there might
eventually be a replacement.
Heathen hordes introduced that opportunity,
devastating civilization
without caring there was no immediate
alternative available.

When history starts to sound too familiar,
foolish ones simply change the channel,
shutting off the lessons of the past.
Corruption soaks into all the barriers
that were meant to stop the ruination,
when no one is first willing to read
the instructions.
So, we go dashing into a destiny
that tried to tell us
curtailment was a better way.
Splurging into decadence
is an open invitation to dig our own graves,
where tombstones will be overrun
by every good intention.
It is another cycle.
It again gives the hordes
a chance to roam.

Air—Err—Heir

Air and heartbeat most closely define
the line between to be and not to be.
I am climbing the stairs without you,
for you have chosen to stay in the dungeon,
far away from deep breathing
and stimulating sunshine.
(you said once the steps were rotten
and I would surely fall through
to crash down on top of you—
another time you said the stairs
led to evil and it was not a
healthy place for anyone to go)
to err is human,
not to err without trying is death;
you added things that
should have been subtracted—
they became obstacles too high to hurdle,
so steps became the only recourse,
advocating an elevated agenda
far above the imprisonment
of which only you are the apparent heir.

You're—Your—Yore

You're the best thing that's ever happened to me,
said I to Silver Spoon.
Help yourself to whatever you want,
was Silver Spoon's reply.
(I love it when she whispers
sweet everythings in my ear).

Helping oneself to another slice of life,
without reaching first for a pocket,
seems like a positive proposition,
especially when it's your chance to dance;
but, when I mentioned it to her,
she said no ring was needed
to bind her to my side,
when Velcro was so cheap.

With everything going so well,
it almost seems like a fairy tale,
but I have never been a frog
in need of kissing, nor a charming prince,
and she has never known
the rags of Cinderella,
so it's best to let a poor boy like me
just start over in a new story,
where we can live happily ever after
by turning pages into a greater tale of yore.

Missed—Mist

Missed objectives
can become opportunities
to succeed the next time,
with better planning
to avoid the now known pitfalls,
and a proper understanding
of how they should reveal themselves
with proper credentials—
but all too soon,
without due diligence,
they're ready to relinquish
their solidity,
and return to mist.

Coarse—Course

Coarse comments occasionally impinge
against certain perceptions of morality;
if you think you can find a place
that no one finds offensive,
build those images into all the mass
you can scramble to accumulate,
because their life-span is short;
toes get trounced
unannounced,
unintended,
uncaring of apologies
or other gyrations;
ultimately, any attempts
to salvage those contents
become mere illusions
of anticipated gains,
having already run their course.

Seize—Sees—Seas

Seize the moment!
Find the obstructing page of hurting words!
Because it is unnerving and
thrusts us sideways without consent,
we must grab it before it can defile—
simple diligence can make the needed
changes from the context.
Find any good it sees inside the sentences,
and rally to that call;

but, since mostly filth and
desecration define its existence,
let's avoid the turmoil,
and obliterate the temptation
by washing over it, to cleanse,
like the multitudinous sands
of the seven seas.

Intense—Intents

Intense negotiations fly words
against opposite sides,
sometimes assigned randomly,
depending on mood or stubbornness;

occasionally, words don't belong there,
some would argue,
pausing briefly to analyze
syntaxes and colloquial tongues;

in the end, neither view wins,
as words subside
into categories of conclusions,
to be filed for a later time
when regurgitating old news
infuriates new agendas
to spew forth into what
was hidden all along,
the words that waged the battle,
contending for the true intents.

Steppes—Steps

Steppes became notorious
as the source of barbarian bands
that ravaged the advanced culture
of the cities,
in return for their gold,
plus enslaving their populations.

The savages brought their own variety
of democracy that was derived
from *might makes right,*
voting themselves as the most popular tyrants,
without ever realizing that their brand
of governance had no word for freedom.

Rebuked, civilization escaped
and took on a new identity, in a new era,
scrambling the details,
but keeping the essence intact.

Acclamations present themselves
to be sacrificed on the altar of accomplishments,
where the blood of others is used
as a substitute for truth, when ultimately,
it is not the rhetoric that describes a culture,
but the abuse of power and subjugating actions
that take the final steps.

Staid—Stayed

Staid countenance
and perplexing outbursts,
without provocation,
were the most prominent flaws
in his otherwise astute accumulation
of noteworthy traits;

gravely aware of these
debilitating features,
present without pride,
he contended silently inside,
a thorn of internal flesh,
secking a solution
within his own torment,
where alone he could not
evict the culprits,

so no one wanted his association,
and it was alone he stayed.

Ware—Wear

Ware is sometimes hard to find,
but in the past,
the nuts and bolts of a final resolution
could be found in the store,
at the corner of the square,
that stocked everything you needed
to make repairs more easy,
with its vast display of hardware.

Ware was invented for forking
the earth's abundance
better than the crudeness
of wood or bone,
so silver spoons,
more malleable and durable,
for a time were common,
but now are only for company,
replaced by everyday plastic
and stainless flatware.

The trade of tinkers was the
repairing of handles and holes
in tin pots and pans,
where the leaking containers
were so common that
it lifted the curse when
they morphed into cast iron
and non-stick cookware.

Just as yesterday's wares
changed to fit a later definition,
hardware became merely an enclosure
for the newest software,
arranging ones and zeros
into frustration,
where the cloud shares
the modern lifestyle that we wear.

Tails—Tales

Tails slap lazily at flies
fond of the summer heat gratuitously
bestowed on the flanks of the cattle;
behind the scenes,
the bull sniffs out new information,
his nose flaring,
and upper lip curling
as if smiling in anticipation
of participating in the conception
of a new generation;
his lifted head evaluates
the accumulated smells
that reveal to him alone
the enticements that lurk,
unfulfilled—
until that perfect instant
when she waits, unperturbed,
and afterwards, simply walks away,
unable to comprehend the natural cycle
that we humans have turned
into convoluted sequences
that brag of undeserved adventures
and the spinning of unrealistic tales.

Fore—For—Four

Fore-grounds feel different than backgrounds—
there is fear close at hand,
forcing indecision to take a stand,
with or without volition;
there is a requirement to somehow react,
NOW!
There are no answers
for easily escaping
because unexpected detours
take you only to places
named Unfamiliar and Lost;
no one seriously contemplates your rescue,
being obsessed with their own detours
and searches to find wisdom
in a world where complications
endorse a theory that two and two
will somehow never equal four.

Presence—Presents

Presence is such a vague concept,
since I am only barely aware of a jumbled mixture
of sounds and sights,
so unstable and unfocused that they
certainly can't be considered as
anything other than a nebulous possibility;
you are located too far east of the center
of energy to be considered as entirely viable
is the strange message that bounces
around insistently inside my head;
suddenly, the sounds shift,
and I suspect the moaning sound is coming from me—
I am trying to ask about my dog, Shep;
then I hear HER voice, softly,
Shep led us to find you dear;
you're in the hospital, after surgery;
don't try to talk now, you're still full of drugs;

I have a clear vision of complex chemical compounds
coursing through my veins,
molecules large enough that they can split apart
and make repairs to my weakened body,
aided by the greatest Healer,
and as I drift away from molecules,
back into the fuzziness of sleep,
I know most of all that I am grateful
for everything God gives to me as presents.

Be—Bee

Be aware that I have been watching,
waiting for my chance.
You have assets that I envy,
but I can't emulate;
some say it's because I'm lazy,
but work doesn't bother me—
some of my best friends are workers.
Being on stand-by is a constant
energy drain,
but my friends feed me well,
and they always seem to know
the best sources,
as they listen to the latest buzz.
It's a boring life for me,
droning on, droning on, drone bee.

Soar—So're—Sore

Soar.
Free bird, soar!
Let no cage be your home.
Let no master call you slave.
Belong to nothing but the air.
Share
your secrets how to fly,
your instincts by how you survive;
if the thermal updrafts are your friends,
so're the clouds where you abide,
glide,
guided by the currents of the wind,
know no boundaries,
nor where feathers fail,
uplifted by hours of tireless air,
fly until the sun sets west;
rest,
for another day, to fly;
rest, let only darkness dispute
any essence of your wings
that might make muscles sore.

Razing—Raising

Razing the landscapes of both
men and nature is what tornadoes do,
twisting trees and churches loose
from foundations that have anchored
their years in faiths of solidarity.

There is a continuing opportunity to expose
the audacity of men's plans to displace
nature first, without ever asking.
There is no retaliation, merely recourse
to the whimsy of the winds.
Building cities in the paths of future twisters
is an ongoing calamity: the infrastructures
just become larger and more predominant,
so demolition echoes the same trend.
As men's efforts spread constantly more
into the domain of nature,
why shouldn't we survivors expect
more loss of life and property?
these are the kinds of questions
we should be raising.

Weights—Waits

Weights on our consciences
are what we try to avoid,
especially before the sun goes down,
but somehow,
glaring actions purposely portray
themselves as absolutely
what needs to be done next,
without realizing that exhibitionists
never seem to get the punchline right anyway;

trading a misplaced agenda
for a walk in the park
isn't as easy as completing the concept;

exchanging adjectives from glaring
to exemplary makes examples
much more worthwhile,
but it isn't as simple as
just speaking the words,
and it's all the misplaced guidance
that stretches veracity too thin
across a chasm that we wish
would shrink on its own,
that makes us reluctant to react,
as temptations tug us sideways
instead of where the straightness waits.

Steel—Steel

Steel floats on water, in the form of boats—
freighters, twelve-hundred feet long, maximum,
if they are to fit through the locks
that re-route part of the St. Marys River
at The Soo, where two Saute Sainte Maries,
towns named the same, face each other
from their opposite international banks
in Canada and Michigan;
the river connects Lake Superior with Huron,
and thus the other lower Lakes,
dropping its elevation by twenty-one feet,
where water sheds itself from two nations
without benefit of a passport;

locking past the cascades,
loads of North American iron ore, coal, and grain
by-pass Chinese containers here,
as they trade places across oceans,
dissipating differences between east and west;
approaching indistinguishable,
as political ideologies merge
towards a central association
where proletariat slaves serve
the universal monied masters,
with allegiances to no nation,
as they accumulate from the workers
of all nations,
everything they can tax,
plus everything they can steal.

Sent—Scent—Cent

Sent as silent reminders to olfactory nerves
intent on sensing and refreshing memories
of emotions from previous times and places,
are smells interconnected with history,
revealing vivid reenactments of:
danger—natural gas
caution—skunk
ill-luck—rotten egg
romance—roses
fun—boat motor exhaust
wrong step—fresh cow pie
toil—sweat
cheer—Christmas wreath
temptation—a box of chocolates
adventure—campfire smoke
convalescence—stale bandages
warm wool blankets—cedar chest
county fair—cotton candy
movies—pop corn
springtime—new-mown lawn

daydreaming;
recollections elicit urges
to pause a moment more,
until the final scent,
to verify historical accuracy;
as I turn over the mental concoctions
of smells while mumbling abstract concepts
of a future poem,
she invites a penny for my thoughts,
but I know I dare not share,
because to her,
they're not worth one red cent.

Red—Read

Red sunsets used to mean
the immediate threat of storms was over,
for sailors, and for me, the farmer,
for the ending of daytime tantrums
that had spent their fury
on lightning tokens
accenting wind and rain.

These days, hued skies merely mean
another layer of pollution
is trying to outdo the splendors of nature,
another man-made fiasco
that should be a story fit only for the fire,
nevermore to be read.

Dew—Due—Do

Dew drips abundantly, at dawn, from all the
side-by-side okra and Smart-weed leaves,
without differentiation or preference;
however, exercising a choice
are the Japanese Beetles
that are clustered on the half-eaten leaves
of the Smart-weed plants,
but have spotted themselves only sporadically,
on the prickly okra, grown for future gumbo;
all the plants are chest-high
to the gardener,
saturating his tee-shirt
as he braves his way everyday
before the July sunlight has yet
to settle on his Alabama garden;
once the sun arrives, the moisture leaves,
as do the beetles,
so the gardener harvests while he can.

The beetles, mostly mating pairs,
have accumulated during the night
onto the Smart-weed leaves they prefer
above those of okra, grapes, roses, and fruit trees,
even the golden silks of sweet corn ears.

How convenient for the gardener,
who walks amongst the plants,
tapping each branch deliberately,
so the dis-lodged beetles
fall faithfully into the soapy container
held below each branch, in turn;
there they perish, instead of flying away
for another chance to demolish crops,
due to the avid attention of the gardener,
trying to save his vegetables
in the least invasive way that he can do.

We'd—Weed
(Take I)

We'd slam doors
with loud proclamations
of who loved who
the most.
It was like a hypocrite
instructing a skeptic
on the finer points
of subjectivity.

Declarations of such disarray
might confound philosophers
into large dissertations,
but inadvertent lessons
made us poor examples
in the guardin' of our children,
where for them,
it was just another weed.

We'd—Weed
(Take II)

We'd really rather not gather
too many mundane projects
into one place and time,
but scattering them
through the hours
makes their burdens less intense,
and adds opportunities
of between ice-tea and
shaking off sun and sweat;
they are the times to procrastinate
the pulling of just one more weed.

Awns—Ons

Awns are the bristly beards
growing on the ends of some
wheat, rye, and barley kernels,
making those grain heads prickly clusters
that are too obnoxious to become a morsel
for the tender-tongued mouths
of the otherwise devastating destruction of deer
looking for an easy meal.

Grain planted in autumn moisture
turns bare-dirt fields
into lush greenness where deer
graze under cover of darkness,
until the dead winter cold
turns everything to brown.
Spring-renewed growth outpaces grazing,
allowing seed stalks to emerge,
rippling with the wind.

As the grain fields are ripening,
and the stalks and heads turn their
succulence of green
into waving amber grain,
the kernels lose their soft milkiness
and harden towards harvest;
this change makes grain heads
more palatable to deer,
but if the heads hold a spikiness,
that deters sensitive mouths,
it saves the crop for a future of bread.
It's just another cycle
of man battling nature,
another iteration of success
measured by simple features
of which varieties develop bristles,
as either offs or ons.

Least—Leased

Least of all, she wanted failure,
so she shopped with care,
and finally found the one.
$E=mc^2$ (hers, entirely theoretical)

She said it was why she married him,
to investigate the intrigues of how
a physicist best used his Energy
to equalize his mass of loneliness
into two living as cheaply as one,
by merely turning on a square flashlight, see?
$E=mc^2$ (his, emerging from frustration)

Countless pages of equations
and screening assumptions as meritorious
only if their view is large enough
to justify throwing away uncertainties
that barely crack the door
behind Einstein's insight and intelligence.
$E=mc^2$ (theory)

where she construed fantasies
to fit inconceivable explanations,
and his insistent explorations
barely hinted at what he hoped he understood,
it left the remainder still as questions,
with both of them wishing that $E=mc^2$
(even in simplest terms)
had more applications of comprehension
than could be bought,
or perhaps even leased.

Rest—Wrest

Rest Areas are anticipated havens,
the coming attractions of interstate highways,
promises of a chance to stretch legs
and relieve certain urgencies
we never can entirely eliminate;
how drastic are the disappointments
when our objectives are
closed due to maintenance,
or for merely mopping!
But, once our attentions are no longer stalled,
the door opens to lesser distractions—
the narrowness of the paper,
non-perforated,
to be pulled apart with randomness
that leaves shreds of undefined edges
fluttering to the floor,
unintended litter of incomplete separations,
interrupting our expectations,
like splintering from the edges of dreams
those goals we wish to wrest.

Wresting—Resting

Wresting distractions from the grasp
of wavering resolutions
matures muscles and builds biceps,
but it doesn't do a thing for a mind
that narrows itself
into the perception
that all is well;
there are consequences that must be acknowledged,
beckonings that demand to be solidified,
and discrepancies that can't be ignored,
before it's time for resting.

Great—Grate

Great as are the aspirations of some,
it becomes easy for them to abuse
what they assume is needful of changing,
such as blessings that befall pathways
intended to be laid-back country roads,
instead of noisy thoroughfares;
those who achieve their destinies early
tend to try to interject their
influences into the circumstances
of those they may inadvertently
consider to be inferior.
It is taking for granted that everything
will always stay the same.

Changes infringe on postulates of those
who know how close they have come to death,
as second chance opportunities entertain
themselves in mundane hospital rooms
that maintain gatherings of idle thoughts.
These are MY thoughts.
This is MY second chance.
Don't blow it!

My prayer is that I will be able
to accommodate acceptance of innocence
as a legitimate alternative
to a previously assumed opinion that
naivety should be viewed with negativity.
Don't blow it!

It is a sifting of concepts:
a shifting towards a finer existence,
as it all becomes the captured essence
of a more close-meshed and eloquent grate.

Weak—Week
(Take I)

Weak from the distress of never knowing
next
what kind of duress I might find
lodged into your debris-filled angst,
I gather strength only from
postulates that the end is near.

I could consider you to be like
the atrocity of asbestos,
with your small fibers intruding
into my breathing, like a cancer
invading the tiny details
of a closed casket called mine.

Certainly I am not so desperate
as to consider an early death
to be a substitute for relief,
but there are no obstacles too
small to ignore,
especially when no one any longer
speaks about details beyond a week.

Weak—Week
(Take II)

Weak beliefs and
feeble instructions
tumbled him into Saturday,
the day God rested,
as the seventh day
of the week.

Lessons—Lessens

Lessons tend to shed themselves
from our minds, sometimes,
causing inferior results
that catapult us into the middle
of forays we'd fought hard to resist,
a persistence of futility,
when priorities get arranged
beyond our control,
so we dare not look away,
lest the future slips past
without our intended influence,
leaving us with scant chances
to advocate our agendas,
as our unfulfilled aspirations
lodge in back seats,
while reality drives home
the differences of what it wants
to emphasize and those things
of which it lessens.

I—Eye—Aye

I should have paid closer attention
to my anchoring,
watched better the tides and
the way the winds changed;
in retrospect, I should have
tried to prolong the time of furled sails,
and kept unhindered the slack chain curving
between the gently rocking prow
and undefined depths,
to fully partake of the safety
inside that contented harbor;

but my negligent eye never caught sight
of the first loose line that first
let the corner of the mainsail slip;
my contentedness never felt the increased
chilling of the breeze, tugging harder—
it never noticed the tightening of the chain,
as more lines broke free,
loosening their holds from the unfurling sails;
for a time, the anchor held fast,
resisting the insistence to release
its hold on an unanticipated destiny,
until, as all the sails were filled
with an unfit wind,
and the anchor dragged
as if it never existed;
so the ship pushed past the harbor,
rushing before the gale of circumstance,
unguided by any captain,
full speed ahead, aye.

Alabama dirt lurks stubbornly under the fingernails of lifetime farmer **Mike Wahl**, accompanied by grease and oil from working on worn-out tractors. For Mike, writing is a more recent passion than farming, but those efforts include a similar association with the reality of grittiness. More time for writing came only after retiring from a 48 year career working as an aerospace engineer, which provided funds to support his farming habit. With writing efforts concentrated primarily on poetry, Mike discovered and joined the Alabama State Poetry Society ASPS), the National Federation of State Poetry Societies (NFSPS), the Huntsville Literary Association (HLA) poetry group, and the Shoals Writer's Guild (SWG). Mike's poems have appeared in numerous print and on-line venues in recent years. This includes a poem in each of the annual anthologies: *Best Poets of 2019: Vol. 5, Best Poets of 2020: Vol. 3,* and the upcoming *Who's Who in American Poetry 2021.* Additionally, in the last five years, Mike has won 32 awards in the ASPS semi-annual contests, and six awards in the NFSPS annual contests. Poem subjects consist of aspects from farming, nature, social issues, politics, religion, and family interactions. This range has been enhanced by serving for several years as a real-beard Santa at a local mall. Mike's first chapbook of poetry, *Living Adverbially,* was published by Finishing Line Press in March 2020, where the titles explore the versatility of adverbs. Another book of poems, *Rooted in Christianity,* was released in September 2021 by Kingdom Winds Press. Mike continues to hone his writing skills in Limestone County, Alabama, where he interfaces daily with family members, livestock, weeds, rocks, and bugs.

www.ingramcontent.com/pod-product-compliance
Lightning Source LLC
Chambersburg PA
CBHW021200090426
42740CB00008B/1173